FRESH TO FREEZER

MW00629607

THINGS YOU'LL NEED

❖ Sharp knives, grater and other cutting utensils

❖ Colander and strainer

❖ Cutting boards

❖ Plenty of water and ice cubes

❖ Wide-mouth funnel

❖ Sturdy, non-reactive saucepans, baking pans and bowls *(such as glass, plastic or stainless steel; avoid aluminum, copper or cast iron)*

❖ Airtight storage containers *(food- and freezer-safe)*, such as tempered glass or rigid plastic containers or heavy-duty zippered plastic bags

❖ Wash rigid containers and lids in hot soapy water and rinse well, or run them through the wash and rinse cycles in an automatic dishwasher

Copyright © 2013 CQ Products
Waverly, IA 50677
All rights reserved.
No part of this book may be reproduced or transmitted in any form or by any means, electronic or mechanical, including photocopying, recording or by any information storage and retrieval system, without permission in writing from the publisher.

Printed in the United States of America
by G&R Publishing Co.

Distributed By:

507 Industrial Street
Waverly, IA 50677

ISBN-13: 978-1-56383-435-6
ISBN-10: 1-56383-435-9
Item #7098

Freezing Basics

Preserving your garden produce in a freezer will yield delicious, fresh-tasting fruits and vegetables all winter long. When properly packaged and frozen, most can be stored for up to one year.

It's best to freeze fruits and vegetables the same day they are harvested. Choose items without bruises, mold or bug damage. Fully ripe produce generally has the best flavor, but for pureed sauces, use slightly overripe fruits and for products that must keep their shape, choose firmer pieces. If you must pick one day and harvest the next, store items unwashed. Wash just before handling.

Most vegetables benefit from blanching to inactivate enzymes that can cause frozen food to deteriorate and lose color, flavor and texture. Food is dropped into boiling water for a short time, chilled quickly and drained before packaging *(see page 4).*

Zippered plastic freezer bags are a good packaging choice for many foods because they can be frozen flat and stacked neatly in the freezer, saving space. Just press out the excess air before sealing them. Vacuum-sealed bags are another excellent choice. But for sauces and other high-liquid items, it may be easier to use rigid containers with tight-fitting lids. Leave ½" to 1" of headspace between the top of the food and the lid to allow for expansion during freezing. To prevent freezer burn, place plastic wrap or crumpled waxed paper over food before sealing.

For convenience, pack produce in easy-to-use quantities that fit your recipes and the size of your family. For example, freeze single servings, 2-cup portions or enough for a whole pie. Label each container with the contents, date and cooking instructions.

Keep your freezer's temperature at 0°F or below for fast, consistent freezing and fewer ice crystals. Place food in the coldest part of the freezer and avoid storing items in the door or near the front where warm air hits them each time the door opens. Keep the freezer relatively full to maintain its cold temperature.

Using the proper techniques and containers will help you enjoy the fruits *(and vegetables)* of your labor for many months.

Freezing Vegetables: Things to Know

How to Blanch Food before Freezing

❖ *Boil food briefly.* Bring a large pot of unsalted water to a full boil over high heat. Lower prepared food into boiling water *(1 lb. or less at a time)* and cover pot for suggested time; begin timing immediately. Food should move around freely in water. Blanching water can be reused several times for multiple batches of the same food.

❖ *Chill food in ice water.* Prepare an ice water bath by filling a clean sink, baking pan or large bowl partway with cold water; add ice cubes. Transfer hot food promptly into the ice water to cool for several minutes to stop the cooking process and retain color. Avoid over-soaking. Replenish ice as needed to keep water cold.

❖ *Drain and pat dry.* As soon as food is cool, remove it from the water and drain in a colander. Spread food on a clean towel and pat until mostly dry. Less water on fruits and vegetables when freezing means fewer ice crystals will form.

❖ *Pack and freeze food.* Pack desired quantity in freezer containers, with like-size pieces together. Label with contents, date and cooking instructions.

Other Helpful Tips

❖ Steam blanching works well for broccoli, pumpkin and winter squash. Boil 1″ to 2″ of water in a pot and place vegetables in a basket 3″ above water. Cover pot and begin timing. It will take about 1½ times longer than water blanching.

❖ Blanching is optional for herbs, onions, peppers and zucchini, especially when used primarily for flavoring.

❖ For soups and other combination dishes that must chill before freezing, set the whole pan in the ice water bath; stir often until cool.

❖ Vegetables with a high water content may get mushy after freezing. Use them in soups, stews and casseroles where a soft texture is acceptable.

❖ Cook most vegetables from the frozen state, using about ½ cup boiling water for every 2 cups vegetables. Exception: cover corn on the cob with water.

Vegetable Preps: 2 Basic Methods

❖ *Blanch and Dry Pack.* Wash, trim and cut vegetables as desired. Blanch and chill in ice water. Drain vegetables well. Pack in freezer containers. Seal, label and store in freezer. Result: It's the quickest method, but pieces may freeze together. Pack in pre-measured quantities for convenience.

❖ *Blanch and Tray Pack (sometimes called individually quick-frozen, tray freezing or flash freezing).* Wash, trim and cut vegetables into pieces as desired. Blanch and chill in ice water. Drain vegetables and pat dry. Spread in a single layer on a rimmed baking sheet. Place in freezer until solid *(about 2 hours)*. Transfer frozen vegetables to freezer containers, seal, label and store in freezer. Result: Vegetable pieces freeze separately so it's easy to scoop out just the amount you need.

Packing & Storage Reminders

❖ Don't overload the freezer with too much room temperature food at once; it slows down the freezing process.

❖ Store similar foods together, placing newest items on the bottom or to the back. Use up older items first.

❖ To avoid freezer burn, remove as much air as possible from packages before sealing by pressing or "burping" containers. Vacuum sealing systems remove all the air to keep food fresh longer. You can also seal a plastic bag, leaving just enough space to insert a drinking straw near one corner; then suck out extra air with the straw and seal completely.

❖ Avoid refreezing items after they have been fully thawed.

FREEZING FRUIT: **Things to Know**

❖ Most fruits may be frozen whole, sliced or pureed. Sort fruit by quality: pieces in peak condition *(fully ripe, no bruising)* are perfect for freezing whole; less-than-perfect pieces can be sliced, discarding damaged parts; and overripe pieces are best when pureed or mashed.

❖ Prepare and freeze each fruit as you wish to use it after thawing. For example, if you plan to use strawberries for shortcake, slice and sweeten them before packaging.

❖ Fruit that is cut and dry packed without sugar should be used within a few months. For longer storage, freeze in water or unsweetened juice.

❖ For convenience, remove stems and fruit pits before freezing.

❖ Package fruits in quantities you'll use at one time.

❖ Some fruits, such as apples and peaches, will darken when exposed to air. After peeling and slicing, dip them into a citric solution like lemon juice or ascorbic-citric powder *(such as Fruit Fresh)* mixed with water. This prevents browning.

❖ Handle fragile fresh fruit gently to avoid bruising.

❖ Don't pick time-sensitive fruit, like berries, until you are ready to prepare them. Leave hulls or stems intact during washing to prevent loss of juices.

❖ Peaches are not as time-sensitive and will soften slightly if allowed to rest at room temperature after picking.

❖ Choose container sizes to fit quantity of food. Full containers will accumulate less frost than half-filled ones.

❖ Serve frozen fruits when they are still partially solid to avoid a mushy texture.

❖ Toss frozen fruit into a blender to add thickness to smoothies, milk shakes and other slushy mixtures.

Fruit Preps: 4 Basic Methods

❖ *Dry or Unsweetened Pack.* Rinse and drain fruit. Slice as desired and fill freezer containers. Seal, label and freeze. Result: It's the quickest way to freeze fruit without sugar. Fruit pieces may freeze together in a clump so pack in pre-measured quantities for convenience. Some fruits benefit from added liquid, such as water.

❖ *Tray Pack (sometimes called individually quick frozen, tray freezing or flash freezing).* Rinse and drain fruit; spread on towels and gently pat dry. Spread fruit in a single layer on a rimmed baking sheet. Place in freezer until solid *(about 2 hours).* Transfer frozen fruit to freezer containers, seal, label and store in freezer. Result: Fruit pieces freeze separately so it's easy to scoop out just what you need.

❖ *Sugar Pack.* Rinse and drain fruit. Slice as desired and mix with sugar. *(This draws out the juice and turns into a syrup that protects fruit.)* Pack in freezer containers, seal, label and freeze. Result: This is especially good for strawberries, raspberries, blackberries and rhubarb. It's an easy way to add sweetness to fruit.

❖ *Syrup Pack.* Prepare a syrup by boiling sugar and water *(or juice)* until dissolved. *(Heavy syrups contain a higher sugar-to-water ratio than lighter syrups.)* Cool completely. Rinse, drain and slice fruit as desired. Pack in freezer containers and pour cold syrup over fruit until covered. Press crumpled waxed paper on top to keep fruit submerged. Seal, label and freeze. Result: It can be served as fruit sauce and works well for pitted fruits like peaches.

❖ *Pureed.* Use a blender or food processor to puree fruit until smooth. Sweeten with sugar, if desired. Pour into freezer containers, leaving headspace. Seal, label and freeze. Result: This smooth versatile sauce is a great way to use overripe fruit.

Asparagus

Harvest in the spring by snapping or cutting young tender spears at ground level when 6˝-9˝ tall and tips are still tightly closed.

FREEZING METHODS

PREP. Wash and sort spears by size. Snap off woody light-colored ends and trim stalks as needed. Cut into even pieces, 1˝-4˝ long. Blanch same-size pieces for 1½-3 minutes and chill in ice water *(see page 4)*.

> 1 lb. asparagus = 15-20 thin spears = 2-3 C. sliced

DRY PACK. Drain blanched, chilled asparagus and pack in freezer containers. Seal, label and freeze.

TRAY PACK. Drain blanched, chilled asparagus and pat dry. Spread pieces in a single layer on a rimmed baking sheet and freeze for 2 hours. Transfer to zippered freezer bags; seal, label and store in freezer.

Quick Look		
	Blanch	1½ -3 minutes *(small spears need less time than large ones)*
	Storage	up to 12 months

Recipes

Asparagus Roll-Ups

- ❖ 20 fresh asparagus spears
- ❖ 1 (8 oz.) pkg. cream cheese, softened
- ❖ ¼ C. Cheddar spread, softened
- ❖ ¼ C. Swiss almond spread, softened
- ❖ 1 egg
- ❖ 1 loaf sandwich bread
- ❖ 1 C. butter, melted
- ❖ Garlic powder, optional

Snap ends off asparagus, leaving spears 5″-7″ long. Blanch for 2 minutes; chill and pat dry as directed. In a medium bowl, whisk together cream cheese, Cheddar spread, almond spread and egg until well-blended; set aside. Cut off bread crusts and discard; roll bread flat with a rolling pin. Spread cheese mixture generously on one side of each bread slice. Lay one asparagus spear on cheese, centered along one edge of bread; roll up. When all are rolled, dip each one in butter and set on a rimmed baking sheet. Freeze at least 1 hour. If desired, cut rolls into thirds. Place roll-ups in freezer containers; seal, label and freeze for up to 3 months. To prepare, arrange desired number of frozen roll-ups on a baking sheet. Bake at 350° for 20 minutes or until golden brown. *Makes 20 full roll-ups.*

Other Ways to Enjoy

- ❖ Add blanched, chilled asparagus to freezable casseroles and soups.

- ❖ Combine blanched asparagus with other blanched vegetables; tray pack and freeze in bags.

Rhubarb

Look for firm crisp stalks, 12"-24" long. Grasp stalks near the base, twist slightly and pull. Cut off and discard leaves.

Freezing Methods

Prep. Wash stalks and pat dry. Cut same-size stalks into even pieces (½"-1") and discard root ends. Blanching is not necessary.

> 1 lb. sliced rhubarb = about 4 C. = 2 C. cooked

Dry Pack. Place sliced rhubarb in freezer containers; seal, label and freeze.

Tray Pack. Spread rhubarb pieces in a single layer on a rimmed baking sheet and freeze for 2 hours. Transfer to freezer containers; seal, label and store in freezer.

Sugar Pack. Mix 4 C. sliced rhubarb with 1 C. sugar; stir until combined and juicy. Place in freezer containers; seal, label and freeze.

Syrup Pack. In a saucepan, combine 2 C. sugar with 4 C. water. Boil and stir until dissolved; cool completely. Fill freezer containers with sliced rhubarb and add syrup until covered, leaving headspace. Press crumpled waxed paper on top. Seal, label and freeze.

Quick Look			
Sugar Pack	4 C. fruit		1 C. sugar
Syrup Pack	4 C. water		2 C. sugar
Storage	6-12 months		

Rhubarb-Peach Freezer Jam

- ❖ 8 C. sliced fresh rhubarb
- ❖ 4 C. sugar
- ❖ 1 (21 oz.) can peach pie filling
- ❖ 1 (3 oz.) pkg. peach or orange gelatin

In a large bowl, combine rhubarb and sugar; stir well. Cover and let stand at least 2 hours or refrigerate overnight. Transfer mixture to a large saucepan and bring to a boil over medium-high heat. Reduce heat and simmer for 10 minutes, stirring occasionally. Meanwhile, dice peaches in filling mixture and add all to saucepan. Return mixture to a boil. Remove from heat and stir in gelatin until dissolved. Ladle jam into small containers, leaving headspace. Cover tightly and cool to room temperature. Let stand until set, up to 24 hours, before placing in freezer. Freeze for up to 1 year. *Makes about 5 cups.*

Rhubarb Sauce

- ❖ 8 C. sliced fresh rhubarb
- ❖ 1 to 1½ C. sugar
- ❖ 1 (3 oz.) pkg. strawberry, cherry or raspberry gelatin, optional

In a large saucepan over medium heat, combine rhubarb, ½ C. water and sugar to taste. Cover and bring to a boil; stir well. Reduce heat and simmer covered for 15 to 20 minutes or until rhubarb is tender and broken down, stirring occasionally. Remove from heat. If desired, stir in gelatin until dissolved. Let cool. Pour into containers, leaving headspace. Freeze for up to 9 months. To use, thaw and serve as a side dish. *Makes about 4½ cups.*

Strawberries

Harvest berries when fully ripe. Look for a bright red color all over, natural shine and fresh-looking green stem caps.

Freezing Methods

Prep. Just before use, rinse berries in cool water, leaving stem caps *(hulls)* intact to retain juices. Pat dry and then remove caps. Separate any soft berries for crushing or pureeing.

> 1 pt. whole strawberries = about 2 C. diced or 1¼ C. crushed
> 1 lb. whole strawberries = about 2⅓ C. sliced

Tray Pack. Spread whole berries in a single layer on a rimmed baking sheet and freeze for 2 hours. Transfer to zippered freezer bags; seal, label and store in freezer.

Unsweetened Pack. Pack sliced or crushed berries in freezer containers. Cover with water or berry juice. If desired, stir in ascorbic acid powder. Press crumpled waxed paper on top to keep fruit submerged. Seal, label and freeze.

Sugar Pack. Halve, slice or crush berries; measure and place in a bowl. Sprinkle ½-1 C. sugar over 4 C. berries. Stir gently until sugar dissolves. Place in freezer containers; seal, label and freeze.

Quick Look			
Sugar Pack	4 C. fruit		½-1 C. sugar
Syrup Pack	4 C. water (or berry juice)		4 C. sugar
Storage	up to 12 months		

SYRUP PACK. In a saucepan, combine equal parts water *(or berry juice)* and sugar, such as 4 C. of each. Boil and stir until dissolved; cool completely. Fill freezer containers with whole or sliced strawberries and add syrup until covered *(approximately ⅓-½ C. syrup for each pint container)*. Press crumpled waxed paper on top. Seal, label and freeze.

RECIPES

Strawberry-Kiwi Salsa

- ❖ *2 kiwifruit*
- ❖ *1 Granny Smith apple, cored*
- ❖ *2 C. diced fresh strawberries*
- ❖ *Juice of 1 lemon*
- ❖ *½ C. brown sugar*
- ❖ *1 T. hot sauce, or to taste*
- ❖ *½-1 tsp. cayenne pepper, or to taste*

Peel and dice kiwifruit and apple into a medium bowl; add strawberries. In a small bowl, mix lemon juice and brown sugar until dissolved. Stir in hot sauce and cayenne pepper. Pour mixture over fruit and toss to coat. Pour into small freezer containers, leaving headspace; freeze for up to 6 months. To use, thaw and serve chilled with chips or meat. *Makes about 3½ cups.*

NOTE *Spices become hotter with time.*

Other Ways to Enjoy

- ❖ Toss frozen strawberries into a blender with other ingredients for smoothies, daiquiris and malts.

Cherries Sweet & Sour

Wait until cherries are fully ripe, slightly softened and have reached their full color before harvesting. Leave stems intact until use.

Freezing Methods

Prep. Rinse and drain cherries. Remove stems and pits; cut cherries in half. Mix with ascorbic-citric powder to preserve best color and flavor.

> 1 lb. whole cherries = about 4 C. = about 2½ C. pitted

Tray Pack. Spread sweet or sour cherries in a single layer on a rimmed baking sheet and freeze for 2 hours. Transfer to zippered freezer bags; seal, label and store in freezer.

Sugar Pack. *(for use in baked desserts)* Mix 4 C. sour cherries with ¾ C. sugar until dissolved. Pack in freezer containers; seal, label and freeze.

NOTE *Bing and Rainier are common sweet cherries; Montmorency is a popular sour cherry.*

Quick Look			
	Sugar Pack *(sour cherries)*	4 C. fruit	¾ C. sugar
	Syrup Pack *(sweet cherries)*	4 C. water	1¼ C. sugar
	Syrup Pack *(sour cherries)*	4 C. water	2⅔-4 C. sugar
	Storage	10-12 months	

SYRUP PACK. *(to serve cherries uncooked)* For sweet cherries, boil 4 C. water with 1¼ C. sugar. For sour cherries, boil 4 C. water with 2⅔-4 C. sugar. Stir to dissolve and let cool. Fill freezer containers with cherries and cover with syrup, leaving headspace. Press crumpled waxed paper on top. Seal, label and freeze.

RECIPES

Cherry Ice Cream Sauce

- ❖ 4 C. halved, pitted sweet cherries
- ❖ 2-2½ C. sugar
- ❖ ½ C. light corn syrup
- ❖ ¼ C. lemon juice
- ❖ 1 (1.75 oz.) pkg. fruit pectin powder

In a large bowl, combine cherries, sugar, corn syrup and lemon juice; let stand for 30 minutes, stirring occasionally. In a small saucepan over medium heat, combine 1 C. water and pectin; boil and stir for 1 minute. Pour over cherry mixture and stir for 3 minutes. Ladle into freezer containers, leaving headspace. Seal and let stand at room temperature until cool. Freeze for up to 1 year. To serve, thaw and spoon over ice cream, yogurt or other desserts. *Makes about 6 cups.*

NOTE *Sour cherries are also called "tart" or "pie" cherries.*

Other Ways to Enjoy

- ❖ Make cherry bruschetta with sweet or tart cherries. Drizzle toasted slices of French bread with olive oil and top with mozzarella cheese and bruschetta.

Blackberries & Raspberries

Let berries ripen fully before picking. Raspberries will come off the core easily, leaving a hollow, but blackberries keep their core.

Freezing Methods

Prep. Just before use, rinse berries and drain well. Remove any stems. Gently pat dry.

> 1 lb. whole blackberries = about 3½ C.
> 1 lb. whole raspberries = 4-4 ½ C. = about 2 C. mashed

Tray Pack. Spread whole berries in a single layer on a rimmed baking sheet and freeze for 2 hours. Transfer to zippered freezer bags; seal, label and freeze.

Sugar Pack. Mix 4 C. whole berries with 1 C. sugar until well coated. Pack in freezer containers; seal, label and freeze.

Syrup pack. Boil 4 C. water *(or berry juice)* with 4 C. sugar. Stir to dissolve and cool completely. Fill freezer containers with whole berries. Cover berries with syrup , leaving headspace. Press crumpled waxed paper on top. Seal, label and freeze.

Quick Look			
Sugar Pack	4 C. whole fruit	1 C. sugar
Syrup Pack	4 C. water	4 C. sugar
Storage	up to 12 months *(use unsweetened berries in 3-6 months)*	

RECIPES

Iced Wine Berries

- ❖ 3 C. quartered fresh strawberries
- ❖ 1 C. fresh blueberries
- ❖ 1 C. fresh blackberries
- ❖ ¼ C. sugar, or more to taste
- ❖ 1 T. finely chopped fresh mint
- ❖ Reisling or Prosecco wine
- ❖ 1 C. fresh raspberries

In a medium bowl, combine strawberries, blueberries and blackberries. Toss with sugar. Add mint and drizzle with enough wine to accumulate 1" in bottom of bowl. Gently fold in raspberries; let stand about 1 hour. Scoop into rigid freezer containers and top with crumpled waxed paper. Seal, label and freeze for up to 3 months. To use, partially thaw and spoon fruit and juice over ice cream or cake; top with whipped cream. *Makes about 5 cups.*

Freezer Raspberry Sauce

- ❖ 3 C. mashed fresh raspberries
- ❖ 3 C. sugar
- ❖ 1 C. light corn syrup
- ❖ 1 (3 oz.) pouch liquid fruit pectin
- ❖ 2 T. lemon juice
- ❖ 4 C. whole fresh raspberries

In a large bowl, mix mashed raspberries, sugar and corn syrup. Let stand for 10 minutes. In a small bowl, mix pectin and lemon juice; add to raspberry mixture and stir for 3 minutes. Gently stir in whole raspberries. Ladle into rigid freezer containers, leaving headspace. Seal and let stand overnight or until partially set. Label and freeze for up to 1 year. To use, thaw and stir. Serve over cake, ice cream, waffles, cheesecake or chicken. *Makes about 8 cups.*

17

Herbs

Harvest herbs in the morning when it's cool. Snip plants throughout summer, but cut off no more than one-third of stem's length each time.

Freezing Methods

Prep. Rinse herbs in cool water and pat dry. To strip off leaves, pull stem through fingers. *(Frozen herbs are best for use in cooked foods.)*

1 T. chopped fresh herbs = about 1 tsp. dried = ½ tsp. ground

Tray Pack. Spread leaves or sprigs in a single layer on a rimmed baking sheet and freeze for 1 hour. Transfer frozen leaves to a zippered freezer bag. Seal, label and store in freezer.

Water Pack. *(cubes)* Mince leaves with kitchen shears. Place

1 T. minced herbs into each ice cube tray opening; fill with water. Freeze about 2 hours. Top off with more water as needed and freeze until solid. Pop cubes into a zippered freezer bag. Seal, label and store in freezer.

Oil Pack. *(cubes)* Mince leaves with kitchen shears. Mix 1 C. herbs with 2-3 T. olive oil. Spoon mixture into ice cube trays and freeze. When firm, pop cubes into a zippered freezer bag. Seal, label and store in freezer.

Quick Look

Storage	up to 12 months

RECIPES

Basil Pesto Cubes

- ½ C. toasted pine nuts
- 4 C. fresh basil leaves, firmly packed
- 2 to 4 cloves garlic, chopped
- ¼ to ½ C. olive oil, plus more to serve
- ½ C. grated Parmesan cheese
- **For later use:** half & half, salt and pepper to taste

With a food processor, puree pine nuts, basil and garlic. Slowly add olive oil and process until smooth. Add Parmesan cheese; pulse until combined. Spoon pesto into ice cube trays, cover and freeze. When solid, pop cubes into zippered freezer bags. Seal, label and freeze for up to 1 year. To use, toss partially thawed cube(s) with hot cooked pasta, rice or vegetables; stir in a little half & half, olive oil, salt and pepper. *(Pesto may also be frozen without the cheese; just add it after thawing.)* Makes about 1 cup.

Other Ways to Enjoy

Freeze herbs in logs by placing 1 C. packed fresh herbs in a quart-size zippered freezer bag and pressing evenly along bottom of bag. Roll bag from bottom to top, compressing leaves into a firm log shape and pressing out air. Fasten with rubber bands; label and store in freezer. To use, remove herb log from bag and slice off desired quantity; rewrap and return to freezer.

Broccoli

Choose dark green, compact broccoli heads with small, tight florets. Cut the stalk 6"-8" below head.

Freezing Methods

Prep. Soak freshly picked broccoli in salted water for 30 minutes to remove pests *(1 T. salt per half-gallon of water)*. Drain and rinse well. Cut off large stalks and reserve for soups, casseroles or stir-frying *(see page 58)*. Cut heads into separate 1"-2" florets; slice small stalks, if desired. Blanch in boiling water for 2-3 minutes *(or steam blanch for 5 minutes)* and chill in ice water *(see page 4)*.

> 1 lb. = about 6 C. broccoli florets

Dry Pack. Drain blanched, chilled broccoli and pack in freezer containers. Seal, label and freeze.

Tray Pack. Drain blanched, chilled broccoli and pat dry. Spread pieces in a single layer on a rimmed baking sheet and freeze for 2 hours. Transfer to zippered freezer bags; seal, label and store in freezer.

Brussels Sprouts. Blanch and freeze like broccoli, but sort by size. Blanch small sprouts 3 minutes; large sprouts 5-6 minutes.

Quick Look		
	Blanch *(with boiling water)*	2-3 minutes
	Blanch *(with steam)*	5 minutes
	Storage	6-12 months

RECIPES

Broccoli-Cheese Soup

❖ 2 T. butter

❖ 1¼ C. chopped onion

❖ 1 tsp. minced garlic

❖ 1 (49.5 oz.) can chicken broth

❖ 9 C. broccoli florets

❖ 1½ C. instant nonfat dry milk

❖ ¼ C. flour

❖ Salt and pepper to taste

❖ 1 C. Velveeta cheese or Cheez Whiz, plus more when reheating

In a large saucepan over medium heat, melt butter. Sauté onion about 4 minutes; add garlic and sauté briefly. Add broth and bring to a boil. Reduce heat, cover and simmer for 5-7 minutes or until broccoli is tender. Remove from heat and let cool 20 minutes. Remove and blend half of mixture to desired consistency. Return to saucepan with remaining soup; set aside. In a bowl, whisk together dry milk and ½ C. warm water to dissolve. Whisk in flour. Gradually mix some warm soup into flour mixture to blend; then stir all into saucepan over low heat. Season with salt and pepper; add cheese. Cook and stir until cheese melts. Serve hot, or chill pan in ice water and divide among freezer containers. Seal, label and freeze for up to 2 months. To prepare, thaw and reheat, whisking in more cheese, salt and pepper to taste. *Makes 9-10 cups.*

Other Ways to Enjoy

❖ Add thawed chopped broccoli to ham and cheese quiche, or stir into hash brown mixtures before baking.

❖ Make and freeze your favorite broccoli-rice casserole. Top with buttered bread crumbs before baking.

Corn

Pick corn when ears are completely filled out and silks are golden. Kernels should be full of sweet, milky juice.

Freezing Methods

Prep. Remove husks and silks. Trim ends of ears as needed. Rinse and sort according to size of kernels. Corn may be blanched on the cob or after cutting.

> 1 medium cob = ½-¾ C. corn kernels

Corn on the Cob. Blanch medium ears in boiling water for 9 minutes *(small ears, 7 minutes; large ears, 11 minutes)*. Chill in ice water, drain and pat dry *(see page 4)*. Wrap each ear in foil and place 4-5 cobs in each large zippered freezer bag. Seal, label and freeze for up to 3 months. To prepare, unwrap ears and spread with soft butter; season with salt and pepper. Rewrap and place on upper oven rack with a baking sheet below to catch drips. Bake at 425° for 25-35 minutes or until done. Frozen ears may also be placed in a pot of cold water and brought to a boil; simmer for 5-10 minutes.

Quick Look		
Blanch *(on cobs)*	7-11 minutes
Blanch *(on cobs & cut)*	4-6 minutes
Raw-Cut *(simmered)*	5-10 minutes
Storage	3-12 months

WHOLE KERNEL CORN. 3 methods

Blanched. *(plain)* Blanch corn on cobs for 4-6 minutes; chill in ice water and drain *(see page 4)*. Over a large bowl, cut kernels off cobs, about ¾ through kernel depth without cutting cob. Tray pack or dry pack in freezer containers. Seal, label and freeze for up to 1 year. To serve, season and cook until hot and tender.

Raw-Cut & Simmered. *(seasoned)* Cut raw corn kernels from cobs and place in a large saucepan. For 4 C. kernels, add ¾ C. water, 1 tsp. salt and 2-4 T. sugar. Bring to a simmer over low heat and cook for 5-10 minutes. Chill pan in ice water, stirring frequently, or transfer corn to large baking pans to chill. Pack in freezer containers; seal, label and freeze for up to 1 year. Reheat to serve.

No-Cook. *(seasoned)* Cut raw corn kernels from cobs. Scoop 10 C. kernels into a large bowl. Stir in ½ C. sugar, 2 T. salt and 2½ C. ice water. Set a gallon-size plastic bag of ice on top of corn mixture to chill for 20 minutes. Scoop 2-cup portions of corn and liquid into quart-size freezer containers; seal, label and freeze. Use within 3 months. To prepare, bring to a boil and then simmer for 10 minutes or until tender.

CREAM-STYLE CORN. Prepare blanched or raw-cut corn as directed above for whole kernel corn, except cut through the center of kernels and then use the back of a knife to scrape remaining corn off cobs with the juice and pulp. Scoop into freezer containers, leaving headspace. Seal, label and freeze for up to 1 year. To prepare, heat corn in a saucepan with half & half and butter; season with salt and pepper.

continued

continued from page 23

Corn & Pepper Chowder

- ❖ 1 T. canola oil
- ❖ 2 C. chopped onion
- ❖ 1½ C. chopped red bell pepper
- ❖ 2 C. grilled corn kernels*
- ❖ 1 (48 oz.) container chicken broth
- ❖ ¾ tsp. dried thyme
- ❖ ⅛-¼ tsp. cayenne pepper
- ❖ **For later use:** chicken bouillon granules, flour, whipping cream, salt and pepper

In a large saucepan over medium heat, heat oil. Add onion and bell pepper; sauté until almost tender. Add corn, broth, thyme and cayenne pepper; bring to a boil. Reduce heat, cover and simmer for 15 minutes. Remove from heat and cool pan in ice water, stirring frequently. Pour into a large freezer container, leaving headspace; freeze. To serve, thaw soup and pour into a large saucepan over medium heat. In a screw-top jar, dissolve 1 tsp. bouillon in 1 C. hot water. Add ½ C. flour; cover and shake well. Stir flour mixture into soup and simmer until slightly thickened and bubbly. Stir in ½-¾ C. cream and heat through. *Makes about 8 cups.*

* To grill, shuck corn and brush kernels with olive oil (or leave corn in husks and soak in cold water for 10 minutes). Place ears on a grate over hot coals and cook for 15-20 minutes or until tender, turning frequently with tongs. Kernels of shucked corn will brown and caramelize; husks will turn brown.

TIP Rub a damp paper towel down the cob to remove pesky silk strands.

Southwestern Corn Salsa

- ¼ C. sliced green onions
- ½ C. diced green bell pepper
- ½ C. diced red or yellow bell pepper
- 2½ C. fresh corn kernels
- ⅓ C. fresh basil, finely chopped
- 1 C. grape tomatoes, coarsely chopped
- 3 T. lime juice
- 3 T. red wine vinegar
- 2 T. olive oil
- 1 tsp. salt
- ¼ tsp. garlic powder
- **For later use:** black beans (rinsed and drained), pepper

In a large bowl, combine onions, green and red bell peppers, corn, basil and tomatoes; set aside. In a small bowl, whisk together lime juice, vinegar, oil, salt and garlic powder; pour dressing over vegetables and toss well. Refrigerate to blend flavors. Then pack in freezer containers, seal, label and freeze for up to 3 months. To serve, thaw completely and stir in about ½ C. black beans to 2 C. salsa. Drain as needed and season with pepper. Serve with chips or meat. *Makes about 4 cups (without beans).*

Other Ways to Enjoy

To freeze corn on the cob quickly, wrap individual unshucked ears of corn in foil and freeze in zippered bags for up to 2 months. To cook, set foil-wrapped ears on a baking sheet in a cold oven. Set oven at 400° to let corn thaw and bake for 1-1¼ hours. To serve, shuck ears with a towel, rinse and serve.

Green Beans

Green bean pods should be young, firm and crisp, with no visible bulges. A bulge indicates the bean is overripe.

Freezing Methods

Prep. Wash in cool water. Trim stem end of beans and cut into even pieces, 1"-4" long. Blanch for 3 minutes and chill in ice water (see page 4). For best results, blanch in batches of same-size pieces.

> 1 lb. trimmed green beans = about 3 C.

Dry Pack. Drain blanched, chilled green beans and pack in freezer containers. Seal, label and freeze.

Tray Pack. Drain blanched, chilled green beans and pat dry. Spread pieces in a single layer on a rimmed baking sheet and freeze for 2 hours. Transfer to zippered freezer bags; seal, label and store in freezer.

Note *Prepare and freeze **yellow wax beans** and **purple snap beans** like green beans. (Purple beans will turn deep green when cooked.)*

Quick Look		
Blanch	3 minutes
Storage	up to 12 months

RECIPES

Garlic Green Beans

- ❖ 8 C. sliced fresh green beans
- ❖ 1 C. toasted pine nuts
- ❖ 2 C. chopped onion
- ❖ 2 tsp. minced garlic
- ❖ *For later use:* olive oil, butter, salt and pepper to taste

Blanch and chill green beans as directed on page 26. Drain well and transfer beans to a large bowl. Add pine nuts, onion and garlic; toss well. Divide mixture and pack 2½-cup portions in freezer containers; seal, label and freeze. To prepare one portion, heat 1 T. oil and 1 T. butter in a large skillet. Add frozen green bean mixture and cook until onions are tender and beans are crisp-tender and hot, stirring frequently. Season with salt and pepper. *Makes about 10 cups.*

NOTE *Harvest **lima beans** while the seeds are green. Wash, shell beans and discard pods. Sort and blanch according to size (2-4 minutes). Chill and freeze like green beans.*

Other Ways to Enjoy

- ❖ Use frozen green beans in place of canned ones to make green bean casserole.

- ❖ Add blanched green beans to freezable casserole recipes; freeze for up to 3 months.

- ❖ Steam frozen green beans until crisp-tender and toss with julienned bell pepper and lemon vinaigrette until coated. Serve warm.

Blueberries

Don't rush to pick these berries. Wait until they're plump and dark blue with a silver sheen. Ripe berries pop off the plant easily.

Freezing Methods

Prep. Sort and remove underripe or overripe berries; pick off any leaves or stems. Rinse blueberries gently in cool water.

> 1 lb. blueberries = about 2⅔ C.

Dry Pack. Drain blueberries thoroughly and pack in freezer containers. Seal, label and freeze.

Tray Pack. Drain blueberries and pat dry. Spread whole berries in a single layer on a rimmed baking sheet and freeze for 1 hour or until solid. Transfer to zippered freezer bags; seal, label and store in freezer.

Tip *Before stirring blueberries into muffin or cake batter, toss them gently with a little flour so they won't sink.*

Quick Look			
Pureed *(sweetened)*	4 C. fruit		1 C. sugar
Storage	up to 12 months *(whole berries are best within 6 months)*		

Recipes

Blueberry Syrup

- ❖ 6½ C. fresh blueberries
- ❖ 2 T. lemon juice
- ❖ 6-7 C. sugar

In a large saucepan, crush one layer of blueberries at a time. Stir in lemon juice. Bring to a boil over medium-high heat; reduce heat to low and simmer for 5-10 minutes or until soft. Pour hot mixture into a wire strainer placed over a large bowl to drain; press gently for additional pulpy juice, if desired. *(When cool, juice may be strained again through cheesecloth for clarified syrup.)* Transfer juice to a large saucepan and stir in sugar. Bring to a boil over medium-high heat. Reduce heat and simmer for 1 minute. Remove from heat and skim off foam. Pour into freezer containers, leaving headspace. Let cool to room temperature. Place in freezer. Thaw completely before using. *Makes 3-4 cups.*

NOTE *For serving size portions, pour prepared syrup into ice cube trays to freeze. When solid, pop cubes into a zippered freezer bag to store in freezer. To serve, thaw out only as many cubes as needed.*

Other Ways to Enjoy

- ❖ Stir partially thawed blueberries into batters for muffins, pancakes, coffee cakes and quick breads.

- ❖ Top hot oatmeal with thawed blueberries, vanilla yogurt and chopped walnuts.

Peaches

Harvest when fruit comes off the tree with only a slight twist. Peaches should be fragrant and have some "give" to the flesh.

Freezing Methods

Prep. Rinse room-temperature peaches. To loosen skins, dip fruit in boiling water for 30 seconds and cool in ice water. Score skin at pointed bud end with an "X"; peel off skin. Halve, remove pit and slice as desired. Add to a bowl with lemon juice or a mixture of water and ascorbic-citric powder *(such as Fruit Fresh)* to prevent browning. Use this method to freeze **nectarines** and **apricots**, too.

> 1 lb. = 3-4 medium peaches = 2½- 3 C. sliced

Tray Pack. Drain sliced treated peaches and pat dry. Spread slices in a single layer on a waxed paper-lined baking sheet; sprinkle with sugar, if desired. Freeze for 2 hours. Transfer frozen peaches to zippered freezer bags; seal, label and store in freezer.

Sugar Pack. Mix 4 C. sliced treated peaches with ⅔ C. sugar; stir to coat and let stand for 10 minutes. Pack in freezer containers, leaving headspace. Seal, label and freeze.

Quick Look			
Sugar Pack	4 C. fruit	⅔ C. sugar
Syrup Pack	4 C. water	2⅔ C. sugar
Storage	up to 12 months *(use tray packed peaches within 3 months)*	

SYRUP PACK. Boil 4 C. water with 2¾ C. sugar, stirring until dissolved; cool completely. Pour ½ C. prepared syrup into freezer containers and add sliced treated peaches, shaking container to pack well. Add more syrup as needed, leaving headspace. Press crumpled waxed paper on top to keep fruit submerged. Seal, label and freeze.

TIP *Another easy prep method: Place whole peaches in the freezer until semi-solid (1-2 hours). This loosens the skin and makes the fruit easier to hold and slice.*

RECIPES

Pureed Peach Sauce

- ❖ *8 fresh peaches*
- ❖ *Ascorbic-citric powder (such as Fruit Fresh)*
- ❖ *¼-½ C. sugar, or to taste*
- ❖ *½ tsp. lemon juice*

Peel, pit and chop peaches into a bowl. Mix ascorbic-citric powder and water following package directions and toss with peaches. Let stand for 5 minutes; drain. In a medium saucepan over medium-high heat, combine peaches and 1 C. water. Bring to a boil; reduce heat and simmer for 5-10 minutes or until soft. Let cool slightly. Using a blender or food processor, puree until smooth. Return to pan and stir in sugar until dissolved. Add lemon juice; let mixture cool. Pour into freezer containers *(or ice cube trays)*, leaving headspace. Seal, label and freeze. To use, thaw and drizzle over ice cream or yogurt, add to smoothies or stir into baked goods for added moisture and sweetness. *Makes about 4 cups.*

NOTE *For chunkier sauce, mash softened peaches with a potato masher instead of pureeing.*

Peppers

All peppers are most flavorful when fully ripe. Look for crisp bright pods without wrinkling. Wear gloves to handle hot peppers.

Freezing Methods

Prep. Wash peppers and pat dry. Cut out stem, white membranes and seeds of sweet bell peppers. Chile peppers may be frozen whole or stemmed, seeded and chopped. Blanching is not necessary unless preparing stuffed peppers.

> **1 large bell pepper = about 1 C. diced**

Dry Pack. Slice or dice sweet bell or hot chile peppers as desired. For easy scooping, place pepper pieces in a single layer in zippered freezer bags. Seal, label and freeze flat.

Blanch & Tray Pack. *(shells)* Cut off tops of bell peppers or slice lengthwise, leaving stem intact, to make "boats." Blanch in boiling water for 1 minute; chill in ice water. Drain and pat dry *(see page 4)*. Set peppers upright on a baking sheet and freeze for 2 hours or until solid. Transfer to freezer containers; seal, label and store in freezer. To use, partially thaw and stuff with your favorite mixture; bake as directed. Blanched shells may also be stuffed before freezing *(see page 33)*.

Blanch	1 minute *(for pepper shells only)*
Storage	8-12 months

Quick Look

Stuffed Mexicali Peppers

- ❖ 6 medium green, red or orange bell peppers
- ❖ 1 lb. cooked taco meat
- ❖ 1 C. salsa
- ❖ 1½ C. cooked rice
- ❖ *For later use:* shredded Cheddar or Monterey-Jack cheese

Leaving stems intact, slice peppers in half from top to bottom to make "boats"; remove seeds and membranes.* Blanch for 1 minute and chill in ice water. Drain and set aside. To cooked taco meat, add salsa and rice. Mix and refrigerate about 20 minutes. Spoon filling into pepper boats. Wrap each filled pepper in plastic wrap and foil; freeze until firm. Transfer to freezer containers to freeze for up to 2 months. To prepare, unwrap peppers and thaw in a casserole dish. Cover and bake at 350° for 25 minutes or until filling is heated through. Top with cheese and bake uncovered 10 minutes more. *Makes 6-12 servings.*

* *For upright shells, slice off tops of peppers; core and seed.*

Other Ways to Enjoy

- ❖ To roast peppers, grill over high heat or broil 5" away from heat until skin is blistered and charred all over, turning frequently. Place hot charred peppers in a covered bowl or tightly closed paper bag to cool and loosen skin. Strip off skin and remove stem, membranes and seeds. Slice as desired and pack in labeled freezer containers.

Zucchini & Squash
SUMMER

Pick young zucchini and yellow squash with thin skins and small seeds, 6"-8" in length and about 2" in diameter.

FREEZING METHODS

Prep. Wash squash. Cut off both ends and discard. If squash is large and more mature, slice in half lengthwise and scrape out seeds.

> 1 medium zucchini = about 2 C. diced, 1¼-1½ C. shredded
> *(lightly packed)* or 8-10 thin "noodles"

Quick Pack. *(shredded)* With skin on, grate raw zucchini and pack 2- or 3-cup portions in zippered freezer bags. Seal, label and freeze. To use, thaw zucchini in a colander to drain juice; press well. Stir into baked recipes. *(This requires less time up front but more time before use.)*

Dry Pack. *(shredded, drained)* With skin on, grate raw zucchini into a colander over a bowl. Sprinkle with salt; mix well and let juice drain into bowl for 30 minutes. Press zucchini to remove more juice, or wrap zucchini in a clean tea towel and twist to squeeze out additional juice.* Pack in freezer containers; seal, label and freeze. *(Zucchini is ready to use when thawed – no draining necessary.)*

Quick Look		
	Blanch	2-3 minutes *(for cubed or sliced only)*
	Storage	up to 12 months

34

BLANCH & DRY PACK. *(cubed or sliced)* Cube or slice unpeeled zucchini or squash. Blanch for 2-3 minutes and chill in ice water *(see page 4)*. Drain and pat dry. Pack in freezer containers; seal, label and freeze.

RECIPES

Zucchini Pizza Crust

- ❖ 3 C. frozen shredded zucchini (thawed, drained, pressed)
- ❖ 2 eggs
- ❖ ⅓ C. flour
- ❖ ½ tsp. salt
- ❖ 1½ tsp. dried oregano, divided
- ❖ Olive oil
- ❖ Shredded cheese
- ❖ Other toppings as desired
- ❖ ½ tsp. dried basil
- ❖ ½ C. grated Parmesan cheese

Preheat oven to 450°. Grease a 12" pizza pan; set aside. In a large bowl, mix zucchini and eggs. Stir in flour and salt. Spread mixture in prepared pan; sprinkle with 1 tsp. oregano. Bake for 8-10 minutes or until firm and lightly browned. Remove from oven and reduce temperature to 350°. Brush crust with oil. Sprinkle with some shredded cheese; add other toppings, remaining ½ tsp. oregano, basil and more shredded cheese. Top with Parmesan cheese. Bake 14-18 minutes more, until cheese is melted. *Makes 1 pizza.*

* Freeze zucchini juice separately for use in soups or stir-fry dishes (see page 61).

continued

Zucchini Noodle Lasagna

- ❖ 2-3 medium zucchini
- ❖ Salt
- ❖ 1 lb. lean ground beef, browned and crumbled
- ❖ 1 tsp. pepper
- ❖ 1 tsp. minced garlic
- ❖ 2 C. thick spaghetti sauce
- ❖ 1 egg
- ❖ 1 (15 oz.) container ricotta cheese
- ❖ 2 T. fresh chopped parsley
- ❖ ¼ C. dry bread crumbs, divided

- ❖ 1 (4 oz.) can sliced mushrooms, drained, divided
- ❖ 3 C. shredded mozzarella cheese, divided
- ❖ ½ C. grated Parmesan cheese, divided

Lightly grease two 5½ x 8" foil pans. Cut off ends of zucchini. With a mandolin or cheese slicer, cut zucchini lengthwise into very thin slices. Arrange zucchini "noodles" in a single layer on a rimmed baking sheet and sprinkle with salt; let "sweat" for 10 minutes. Blot dry with paper towels. *(If desired, tray pack the noodles now, with waxed paper between layers. Do not thaw before use.)* In a large skillet over low heat, combine browned beef, pepper, garlic and spaghetti sauce; remove from heat. In a bowl, mix egg, ricotta cheese and parsley. To assemble, spread a generous ½ C. meat mixture in each prepared pan. Sprinkle with bread crumbs and top with a layer of zucchini noodles. Spread 3 T. ricotta mixture over noodles, followed by a few mushrooms and ½ C. mozzarella cheese. Repeat layers twice, omitting mushrooms on third layer. Top each pan with ¼ C. Parmesan cheese. Cover with foil, label and freeze for up to 3 months. To prepare, thaw in refrigerator and bake at 325° for 45 minutes. Uncover and bake at 350° for 15 minutes more or until bubbly. Let stand 15 minutes before cutting. *Makes 2 small pans.*

Zucchini

Freezer Zucchini Bread

- ❖ 3 eggs
- ❖ 1 C. vegetable oil
- ❖ 2¼ C. sugar
- ❖ 2 C. shredded zucchini
- ❖ 1 T. vanilla extract
- ❖ 3 C. flour
- ❖ 1 T. ground cinnamon
- ❖ 1 tsp. salt
- ❖ 1 tsp. baking soda
- ❖ 1 tsp. baking powder
- ❖ 1 C. chopped walnuts or pecans, optional
- ❖ Powdered sugar glaze

Preheat oven to 350°. Grease and flour two 8" loaf pans; set aside. In a large bowl, beat together eggs, oil, sugar, zucchini and vanilla until well blended. In another bowl, sift together flour, cinnamon, salt, baking soda and baking powder. Add flour mixture to zucchini mixture and mix well. Fold in walnuts, if desired. Divide batter between prepared pans. Bake about 1 hour or until bread tests done with a toothpick. Cool completely. Make a thick glaze of water, vanilla extract and powdered sugar. Drizzle over bread and let dry. Wrap in foil and place in zippered freezer bags to store in freezer for up to 1 year. Thaw before slicing. *Makes 2 loaves.*

Other Ways to Enjoy

- ❖ Add shredded zucchini to meatloaf mixtures or muffin and cake batters *(like chocolate or carrot cake).*

Tomatoes

Tomatoes taste best when left on the vine until fully ripe. Pick when skin is firm and deep red. Flesh should give slightly when pressed.

Freezing Methods

Prep. Wash and blanch whole tomatoes for 30-60 seconds and chill in ice water *(see page 4)*. Remove stems and core; peel off skin.

> 1 lb. = 3-4 medium tomatoes or 5 Romas

Dry Pack. *(raw)* Leave tomatoes whole or quarter or dice them. Pack in freezer containers; seal, label and freeze. *(Sliced Romas may be tray packed raw for use on pizza or to garnish baked dishes.)*

Simple Juice. *(cooked)* Skip blanching and peeling. Cut tomatoes in wedges and simmer in a saucepan for 10-15 minutes. Press through a sieve or food mill, catching juice below. Add salt to taste; let cool. Pour into freezer containers, leaving headspace. Seal, label and freeze.

Stewed. Peel and quarter tomatoes into a saucepan. Cover and cook over medium-low heat for 10-20 minutes until tender. Chill pan in ice water. Pack in freezer containers, leaving headspace. Seal, label and freeze.

Quick Look		
	Blanch	30-60 seconds
	Storage	up to 12 months

Recipes

Basic Freezer Tomato Sauce

- ❖ 8 lbs. plum (Roma) tomatoes
- ❖ ¼ C. olive oil
- ❖ ¾ C. finely chopped shallots
- ❖ 4-8 cloves garlic, minced
- ❖ 1 tsp. kosher salt
- ❖ 5 T. chopped fresh basil
- ❖ 2 tsp. brown sugar
- ❖ Salt and pepper to taste

Place tomatoes in a large pot with ½ C. water. Crumple a 15″ piece of parchment paper and dampen with cold water; set flattened paper over tomatoes. Cover pot and cook over low heat for 30 minutes, allowing tomatoes to steam; shake pot occasionally to stir but do not remove lid. Working in batches, transfer tomatoes to a food processor and puree until smooth. If desired, press mixture through a sieve to collect juice and fine pulp in a bowl; discard skin and seeds. Pour mixture into a large pot. Add oil, shallots, garlic, salt and basil. Bring mixture to a boil, reduce heat and simmer uncovered for 40-60 minutes, stirring often, until reduced by about half. Stir in brown sugar and season with salt and pepper. Chill pot in ice water, stirring often. Pour into freezer containers, leaving headspace. Seal, label and freeze for up to 1 year. To use, thaw sauce and simmer for 5 minutes or until heated through. *Makes about 5 cups.*

TRY *Add Italian herbs for Italian dishes; stir in green chiles and crushed red pepper to add heat to Mexican dishes; or increase the basil and garlic or add rosemary or thyme for Mediterranean cooking.*

continued

Freezer Spaghetti Sauce

- ❖ ¼ C. olive oil
- ❖ 2 C. chopped onion
- ❖ 2 tsp. minced garlic
- ❖ 3 lbs. tomatoes, peeled and pureed (about 5½ C.)
- ❖ 3 (6 oz.) cans tomato paste
- ❖ 2 tsp. salt
- ❖ ½ tsp. pepper
- ❖ ½ tsp. garlic salt
- ❖ 3 T. fresh snipped basil (or 1 T. dried)
- ❖ 3 T. fresh snipped oregano (or 1 T. dried)
- ❖ 6 T. fresh snipped parsley (or 2 T. dried)
- ❖ 2 tsp. sugar
- ❖ 1 tsp. brown sugar
- ❖ 2 bay leaves, optional

In a large pot over medium-high heat, heat oil. Add onion and sauté until tender. Stir in garlic and cook until fragrant, about 1 minute. Reduce heat to medium and add 1 C. water, pureed tomatoes, tomato paste, salt, pepper, garlic salt, basil, oregano, parsley, sugar, brown sugar and bay leaf, if desired. When mixture simmers, reduce heat and simmer uncovered for 1-1½ hours or to desired thickness, stirring often. Chill pot in ice water, stirring often. Pour into freezer containers, leaving headspace. Seal, label and freeze for up to 1 year. To use, thaw sauce and simmer for 10 minutes or until heated through. *Makes 7-8 cups.*

TRY *Add diced celery while cooking sauce. You may also add cooked, drained ground beef to sauce during the last 20 minutes of cooking; freeze as directed.*

Tomatoes

Cooked Garden Salsa

- ❖ 3 lbs. plum (Roma) or other tomatoes, chopped
- ❖ 1 (6 oz.) can tomato paste
- ❖ 2½ C. chopped onion
- ❖ 1-2 cloves garlic, minced
- ❖ 2 bell peppers (any color), seeded and chopped
- ❖ 1-3 jalapeño peppers, seeded and chopped
- ❖ 1-3 banana peppers, seeded and chopped
- ❖ 1½ tsp. dried parsley
- ❖ 1 tsp. dried oregano
- ❖ ½ tsp. dried basil

- ❖ ½ tsp. ground cumin
- ❖ ½ tsp. chili powder
- ❖ 1½ tsp. salt
- ❖ ½ tsp. pepper
- ❖ 1-2 tsp. hot pepper sauce
- ❖ 1 tsp. chopped fresh cilantro

In a large bowl, combine tomatoes, tomato paste, ¼ C. water, onion, garlic, bell peppers, jalapeño and banana peppers, parsley, oregano, basil, cumin, chili powder, salt, pepper, hot pepper sauce and cilantro. Mix well. For smoother salsa, pulse mixture in a food processor to desired consistency. Transfer to a large pot over medium heat and bring to a boil. Reduce heat to low and simmer uncovered until thick, 1½-2 hours. Chill pot in ice water, stirring often. Spoon into freezer containers, leaving headspace. Seal, label and freeze for up to 1 year. Thaw and stir before using. *Makes about 5½ cups.*

NOTE *Fresh (uncooked) salsa may be frozen, but it becomes watery when thawed. For best results, drain well before serving or blend mixture before freezing.*

Carrots

Begin harvesting when carrots reach ½" in diameter. Generally, younger carrots are juicier, sweeter and more tender.

Freezing Methods

Prep. Remove tops and scrub carrots with cool water. Peel, if desired. Cut large carrots into coins, cubes or finger-length sticks. Small carrots may be left whole. Blanch pieces for 2 minutes and small whole carrots for 5 minutes; chill in ice water *(see page 4)*.

> 1 lb. = about 5 large carrots = 2½ C. sliced/shredded

Dry Pack. Drain blanched, chilled carrots and pack in freezer containers. Seal, label and freeze.

Tray Pack. Drain blanched, chilled carrots and pat dry. Spread pieces in a single layer on a rimmed baking sheet and freeze for 2 hours. Transfer to freezer containers; seal, label and store in freezer.

Parsnips. Peel and cut off ends; slice as desired. Blanch for 3 minutes; chill in ice water. Drain and pat dry. Pack and freeze like carrots.

Quick Look		
	Blanch	2 minutes *(pieces)*, 5 minutes *(small whole)*
	Storage	up to 9 months

RECIPES

Golden Glazed Carrots

- ❖ 3 lbs. peeled carrots
- ❖ 3 T. flour
- ❖ ½ C. brown sugar
- ❖ 1 tsp. salt
- ❖ ½ tsp. ground thyme
- ❖ 1-2 T. apple cider vinegar
- ❖ 2 T. lemon juice
- ❖ 1 C. orange juice
- ❖ Zest of 2 oranges
- ❖ ¼ C. butter

Slice carrots in 2½" lengths and quarter. Blanch in boiling water for 5 minutes. Drain and rinse with cold water; set aside. In a saucepan, combine flour, brown sugar, salt and thyme. Stir in vinegar, lemon juice, orange juice and zest. Bring to a boil, whisking until creamy. Add butter, reduce heat and cook for 5 minutes, stirring frequently. Line casserole dishes with two layers of foil, extending 5" beyond rim. Divide carrots among prepared dishes and drizzle with sauce; freeze until solid. Remove from freezer and wrap foil around carrots. Lift foil packs from dishes and store in zippered freezer bags for up to 4 months. To prepare, unwrap frozen carrots and set in sprayed casserole dish. Cover and bake at 350° for 30 minutes. Uncover, stir and bake 15 minutes more. *Makes 8-10 cups.*

NOTE *Try the foil liner method to freeze other vegetable dishes, or use foil pans to bake and freeze casseroles or even frosted carrot cake.*

Potatoes

"New" potatoes are harvested when they are small, but the main crop should be dug up after the plant tops die down.

Freezing Methods

Prep. Scrub potatoes with cool water.

> 1 lb. = 3-4 medium potatoes = 2¼ C. diced or 3 C. shredded

Blanch & Dry Pack. *(diced or chunked)* Peel and rinse potatoes. Cut into cubes. Blanch for 2 minutes and chill in ice water *(see page 4)*. Drain well and pat dry. Pack in freezer containers; seal, label and freeze. To use, add to soups or fry in oil.

Blanch, Fry & Dry Pack. *(French fries)* Cut peeled or unpeeled potatoes into ⅜"-½" square strips with knife or crinkle cutter. Blanch for 2 minutes and chill in ice water *(see page 4)*. Drain and pat dry. In a deep-fat fryer set at 375°, partially fry small batches until lightly browned. Drain, cool and pack in zippered freezer bags. Seal, label and freeze. To prepare, deep-fry frozen French fries in 375° oil or oven-bake at 425° until golden brown.

Quick Look		
Blanch	2 minutes
Bake	1½ hours
Storage	8-12 months

Bake & Tray Pack. *(shredded hash browns)* Poke potato skins. Bake at 350° for 1¼ hours; cool completely. Peel and shred potatoes. Spread in a single layer on a parchment paper-lined baking sheet and freeze for 2 hours. Transfer potatoes to zippered freezer bags to store in freezer *(flatten 1 lb. shredded potatoes in each gallon-size bag).* To prepare, fry frozen hash browns in oil or butter until golden brown and slightly crisp. The baking method may also be used for diced, chunked or whole potatoes instead of blanching.

Sweet Potatoes. Brush whole sweet potatoes with oil and bake until tender. When cool, wrap in foil and freeze in plastic bags. Or, puree the sweet potato flesh with a little sugar, water and lemon juice. Pack puree in freezer containers; seal, label and freeze.

Recipes

Chili Cheese Fries

- ❖ *1 lb. homemade frozen French fries*
- ❖ *1 (16 oz.) can chili with beans*
- ❖ *½ C. shredded Cheddar cheese*
- ❖ *Sliced green onions, optional*

Fry potatoes in small batches in 375° oil for 2-3 minutes or oven-bake on a lined baking sheet at 425° for 10-15 minutes, until golden brown. Season as desired. Heat chili in the microwave and spread over hot French fries; sprinkle with cheese and let melt. Top with green onions, if desired. Serve warm. *Makes 4-6 servings.*

Note *Use homemade frozen hash browns to make potato soup quickly. Add bacon, onion and other seasonings as usual.*

Apples

Ripe apples should be crisp and juicy, with dark brown seeds. Pick each variety when they have reached full color.

Freezing Methods

Prep. Wash apples well. Peel, core and cut into even slices or chunks. Soak in ascorbic-citric solution or lemon juice to prevent browning.

> 3-4 medium apples = 1 lb.

Dry Pack. *(unsweetened)* Drain treated apple pieces and pat dry. Pack in zippered freezer bags; seal, label and freeze. *(Unsweetened apples may also be packed in water or unsweetened apple juice.)*

Sugar Pack. *(for baking)* Cut apples into thin even slices. Mix 4 C. sliced apples with ½ C. sugar; stir to coat. Pack in freezer containers; seal, label and freeze. *(For convenient pie-baking, freeze apples inside a pie plate as directed on page 54.)*

Syrup Pack. Boil 4 C. water with 2¾ C. sugar; stir to dissolve. Cool completely. Fill freezer containers partway with cold syrup; pack with apples and cover with more syrup. Press crumpled waxed paper on top to keep fruit submerged. Seal, label and freeze.

Quick Look			
Sugar Pack	4 C. fruit	½ C. sugar
Syrup Pack	4 C. water	2¾ C. sugar
Storage	up to 12 months	

RECIPES

Spiced Apple Rings

❖ 4 lbs. firm, tart apples, peeled and cored

❖ 2 qts. water/2 T. lemon juice

❖ 4 C. sugar

❖ ½ C. red cinnamon candies

❖ ⅓ C. distilled white vinegar

❖ 1 T. whole cloves

❖ 2 drops red food coloring

Slice apples into rings, about ⅜" thick; soak in water/lemon juice. Meanwhile, in a large pot over high heat, combine 2 C. water, sugar, candies, vinegar, cloves and food coloring; bring to a boil. Reduce heat and simmer for 3 minutes, stirring often. Drain apples and add to hot syrup, turning to coat. Simmer for 5 minutes. Strain syrup into a bowl; let apples and syrup cool. Pack apple rings into containers, discarding cloves. Add syrup, leaving headspace. Press crumpled waxed paper on top; seal, label and freeze. Thaw before using. *Makes 8-10 cups.*

Other Ways to Enjoy

❖ To freeze homemade applesauce, peel and slice 3-4 lbs. cooking apples into a pot with 1 cup water and 2 T. lemon juice. Cover and simmer until very tender, 15-20 minutes. Mash and stir in sugar and cinnamon to taste, adding more water as needed. Let cool. Pour into freezer containers, leaving headspace; freeze.

❖ Try Cortland, Granny Smith, Jonathan, McIntosh, Fuji, Gala, Ida Red, Pippin or Winesap apples for cooking and baking.

Beets

Harvest beets that are 1"-3" in diameter, when shoulders protrude from the soil. Look for a dark color and smooth surface.

Freezing Methods

Prep. Clip off beet stems to about 1". Leave tap roots in place and scrub clean under cool water. *(Do not peel before cooking or color and flavor will "bleed" into water.)* In a large pot, cover beets with water and bring to a boil over high heat. Reduce heat, cover pot and simmer for 20 minutes or until fork tender. Chill beets in ice water. Slice off stem and root; peel by rubbing off skin under running water.

1 lb. trimmed = 5 medium beets = about 2½ C. chopped

Dry Pack. Dice, slice or shred cooked, peeled beets. Pack in freezer containers. Seal, label and freeze.

Note *Red beets are most common, but golden and striped beets are also available.*

Simmer	about 20 minutes
Storage	up to 12 months

Quick Look

RECIPES

Beet 'n' Blueberry Muffins

- ❖ 1 C. flour
- ❖ 1½ C. whole wheat flour
- ❖ 1½ C. quick-cooking oats
- ❖ 1 T. baking powder
- ❖ 2½ tsp. baking soda
- ❖ 2 tsp. ground cinnamon
- ❖ 1 tsp. salt
- ❖ 1 C. vegetable oil
- ❖ 2 C. applesauce
- ❖ 1 C. sugar
- ❖ 2 eggs
- ❖ 1 C. fresh or frozen blueberries
- ❖ 1 C. frozen shredded, peeled beets, thawed

Preheat oven to 350°. Lightly grease 24 standard muffin cups or use paper liners; set aside. In a large bowl, combine flour, whole wheat flour, oats, baking powder, baking soda, cinnamon and salt. In another bowl, mix oil, applesauce, sugar, eggs and ½ C. water until well blended. Pour applesauce mixture into flour mixture and stir to blend. Fold in blueberries and beets. Spoon batter into prepared muffin cups. Bake for 22-26 minutes or until muffins test done with a toothpick. *Makes 24 muffins.*

NOTE *Bake mini muffins for 10-12 minutes. (These muffins freeze well.)*

Other Ways to Enjoy

- ❖ To freeze Harvard Beets, boil ¼ C. water, ½ C. sugar, 1½ tsp. cornstarch and ¼ C. cider vinegar for 5 minutes. Toss with 3 C. diced, cooked beets, pack and freeze. To prepare, reheat with 2 T. butter. Freeze for up to 3 months.

Cauliflower

Mature heads of common cauliflower are compact, white and 6"-12" in diameter. To harvest, cut through the stem underneath head.

FREEZING METHODS

Prep. Soak freshly picked cauliflower in salted water for 30 minutes to remove pests *(2 T. salt per gallon of water)*. Drain and rinse well. Cut into 1" floret pieces. Add 1 T. lemon juice to blanching water to maintain white color; blanch for 3 minutes. Chill in ice water *(see page 4)*.

> **1 medium head = 5-6 C. cauliflower florets**

Dry Pack. Drain blanched, chilled cauliflower and pack in zippered freezer bags. Seal, label and freeze.

Tray Pack. Drain blanched, chilled cauliflower and pat dry. Spread pieces in a single layer on a rimmed baking sheet and freeze for 2 hours. Transfer to zippered freezer bags; seal, label and store in freezer.

Quick Look		
	Blanch	3 minutes
	Storage	up to 12 months

Recipes

Loaded Baked Cauliflower

- ❖ 5 C. fresh or frozen cauliflower florets, thawed
- ❖ 1 C. sour cream
- ❖ 1¼ C. shredded Cheddar cheese
- ❖ 5 green onions, sliced
- ❖ 6 T. cooked crumbled bacon
- ❖ Salt and pepper to taste
- ❖ *For later use:* additional Cheddar cheese, bacon, green onions

Cook cauliflower until very tender; drain and finely chop or mash. Let cool. In a medium bowl, mix sour cream, cheese, green onions and bacon. Add cauliflower and stir to combine. Season with salt and pepper. Pack in freezable baking dish*(es)*. Seal, label and freeze for up to 3 months. To prepare, thaw overnight in refrigerator. Uncover and sprinkle with additional cheese and bacon. Bake at 350° for 20-30 minutes or until bubbly and heated through. Sprinkle with more green onions before serving. *Makes about 7 cups.*

Other Ways to Enjoy

- ❖ Toss 6 C. fresh cauliflower florets with canola oil, minced garlic, salt, pepper and Parmesan cheese to taste. Spread on a foil-lined baking sheet and oven-roast at 425° for 20 minutes or until lightly browned and crisp-tender. Turn once during roasting. Cool, pack and freeze. Reheat before serving.

Pumpkin & Squash *Winter*

Pick when fully ripe, solid and heavy, around the time of the first frost. Look for dull-colored, hard rinds.

Freezing Methods

Prep. Scrub clean with cool water. Pierce skin all over with a knife. Bake acorn and other small squash whole at 350° for 50 to 70 minutes or until tender. Microwave large squash *(like butternut)* and pie pumpkins for 3 minutes to soften slightly; then cut in half and scoop out seeds and stringy membranes. Place cut side down in a shallow baking dish; add ¼" water. Cover with foil and bake at 350° until soft and tender, 1¼-1½ hours. When cool enough to handle, cut whole squash in half and scoop out seeds and membranes.

> 1 medium pie pumpkin = about 5 lbs. = 5-6 C. pureed
> 1 large butternut squash = about 4 lbs. = about 4 C. mashed
> 1 medium acorn squash = 2-3 C. mashed

Pureed. Scoop cooked squash or pumpkin flesh from rinds. *(Often, rinds can be lifted cleanly away from cooked flesh.)* Mash flesh or puree with a food processor until smooth. If desired, add ½ C. sugar to every 3 C. pureed pumpkin. Cool completely. Pack in freezer containers; seal, label and freeze.

Quick Look		
	Bake	50 minutes to 1½ hours *(according to size)*
	Storage	up to 12 months

RECIPES

Cranberry Pumpkin Bread

- ❖ 1¾ C. pumpkin puree
- ❖ 4 eggs
- ❖ ½ C. vegetable oil
- ❖ 3¾ C. flour
- ❖ 3 C. sugar
- ❖ 4 tsp. pumpkin pie spice
- ❖ 2 tsp. baking soda
- ❖ 1 tsp. salt
- ❖ 1 C. chopped walnuts or pecans
- ❖ 2 C. fresh or frozen cranberries, thawed, coarsely chopped

Preheat oven to 350°. Grease 2 or 3 standard loaf pans; set aside. In a medium bowl, whisk together pumpkin, eggs and oil. In a large bowl, combine flour, sugar, spice, baking soda and salt. Add pumpkin mixture to flour mixture and stir until moistened. Fold in walnuts and cranberries. Divide batter among prepared pans; bake for 55-65 minutes or until bread tests done with a toothpick. Cool for 10 minutes before removing bread from pans; cool completely. Wrap in foil and place in zippered freezer bags to store in freezer for up to 6 months. Thaw before slicing. *Makes 3 loaves.*

Other Ways to Enjoy

- ❖ For make-ahead pumpkin pie filling, prepare a standard pumpkin filling *(with evaporated milk, egg, etc.)* using about 2 C. cooked pureed pumpkin. Pour into a quart-size freezer container *(each 9" pie crust will hold 3½-4 C. filling)*. Seal, label and freeze. To use, thaw in refrigerator and pour into prepared crust; bake and cool as directed.

Pies

Mix ripe fruit with sugar, thickener and spices, then freeze these delicious fillings in pie plates for convenient pie-baking anytime.

FREEZING METHODS

Prep. Wash, peel and slice fruit as needed *(leave blueberries whole)*. Mix pie filling as directed in each recipe (pages 55-56).

TRAY PACK PIE FILLING. *(standard pies)* Line a 9" pie plate with foil and plastic wrap. Spread prepared filling in lined plate. Freeze uncovered until solid *(at least 4 hours)*. When frozen, remove filling from plate and wrap well with foil; transfer to zippered freezer bag to store in freezer.

TRAY PACK HAND PIES. *(unbaked)* For 16 hand pies, prepare ½ recipe of pie filling, chopping fruit in small pieces. Follow directions on page 57 to assemble hand pies, but do not bake. Set pies on parchment paper-lined baking sheets and freeze for 2 hours. When solid, wrap in foil and transfer to zippered freezer bags to store in freezer.

Quick Look	
Storage	up to 12 months

Peach Pie Filling

- ❖ 4 C. peeled, sliced peaches
- ❖ 1½ T. lemon juice
- ❖ ¼ C. instant tapioca
- ❖ 1 C. sugar
- ❖ Dash of ground nutmeg
- ❖ ⅛ tsp. ground cinnamon

In a medium bowl, toss peaches with lemon juice. Stir in tapioca, sugar, nutmeg and cinnamon; toss until sugar is mostly dissolved. Let stand for 15 minutes. Spread filling in lined pie plate and freeze as directed for tray pack filling *(standard pies)*. To assemble and bake, follow instructions on page 57. *Makes 1 (9″) pie.*

Cherry Pie Filling

- ❖ 1 to 1½ C. sugar, or to taste
- ❖ 4 C. sour cherries, pitted and halved
- ❖ 3 T. instant tapioca
- ❖ 2 T. lemon juice
- ❖ ¼ tsp. salt
- ❖ ½ tsp. almond extract, optional

In a large bowl, mix sugar, cherries, tapioca, lemon juice, salt and almond extract, if desired. Let stand for 15 minutes. Pour filling into lined pie plate and freeze as directed for tray pack filling *(standard pies)*. To assemble and bake, follow instructions on page 57. *Makes 1 (9″) pie.*

continued

continued from page 55

Blueberry Pie Filling

❖ 4 C. fresh blueberries, divided
❖ ½ to ¾ C. sugar
❖ ⅛ tsp. salt
❖ 5 T. arrowroot flour
❖ 1 T. orange juice
❖ 1 tsp. orange zest

Wash blueberries and pat dry. In a small bowl, mash half the berries; set aside. In a medium bowl, mix sugar, salt and flour. Add orange juice, orange zest and mashed blueberries; stir well and let stand for 15 minutes. Fold in remaining whole blueberries. Pour filling into lined pie plate and freeze as directed for tray pack filling *(standard pies)*. To assemble and bake, follow instructions on page 57. *Makes 1 (9″) pie.*

Apple Pie Filling

❖ 5 C. peeled, thinly sliced apples (such as McIntosh)
❖ 2 tsp. lemon juice
❖ ½ C. sugar
❖ ¼ C. brown sugar
❖ ¼ tsp. salt
❖ 2 T. flour
❖ 1 tsp. ground cinnamon
❖ ¼ tsp. ground nutmeg

In a large bowl, toss apples with lemon juice. In a separate bowl, mix sugar, brown sugar, salt, flour, cinnamon and nutmeg. Add sugar mixture to apples and stir to coat. Spread filling in lined pie plate and freeze as directed for tray pack filling *(standard pies)*. To assemble and bake, follow instructions on page 57. *Makes 1 (9″) pie.*

Pies

Assemble. You'll need:

- ❖ 1 (15 oz.) pkg. refrigerated pie crusts or homemade pastry (2 crusts)
- ❖ Butter
- ❖ Milk
- ❖ Sugar

Standard pies: Line a 9″ pie plate with 1 crust. Set unwrapped frozen fruit filling into crust; dot with butter. Top with remaining crust; seal and flute edges. Brush with milk and sprinkle with sugar. Cut vents in top *(or make lattice top or crumb topping*)*. Bake.

Hand pies: From each crust, cut 7-8 circles with a 5″ cookie cutter, rerolling scraps. Place 1½ T. fruit filling on each circle. Brush edges with water and fold in half. Seal edges together with a fork. Brush with milk and sprinkle with sugar. Bake now or freeze as directed on page 54.

* Crumb topping: Omit top crust. Mix ½ C. flour, ½ C. brown sugar and ¼ tsp. ground cinnamon. Cut in 3 T. butter until crumbly. Sprinkle over pie filling in crust and bake as directed.

Bake. Preheat oven to 375°. Bake until crusts are golden brown and filling is bubbly.

Standard pies: Set pie on a baking sheet to catch any spills. Cover with foil and bake for 30 minutes; uncover and bake 40 to 55 minutes longer. If necessary, shield edges with foil and reduce oven temperature to 350° near end of baking time to prevent overbrowning. Cool before cutting.

Hand pies: Poke holes in top crusts. Bake on parchment paper-lined baking sheet for 30 to 35 minutes. Cool slightly and drizzle with icing.

Veggie Combos

Here's the scoop: Freeze fresh vegetables in bags and scoop out just the right amount for soups, casseroles and stir-fries.

Freezing Methods

Prepare individual vegetables as directed below. Fill zippered freezer bags with single vegetables or combine them as desired. Flatten bags and press out air; seal, label and stack in freezer. Most vegetables do not need to be thawed before use. Simply remove the quantity needed for recipes and return bag to freezer.

Bell Peppers. Wash and core peppers; remove membranes. Slice or dice as desired *(no blanching needed when used as flavoring)*. Pack and freeze.

Broccoli. After removing florets, prep the stalks. Cut off and discard woody parts; peel off outer layer and dice or julienne remaining portion. Blanch for 2 to 3 minutes; chill in ice water. Drain and pat dry. Pack and freeze.

Cabbage. Wash and discard outer leaves. Cut into coarse shreds or thin wedges. Blanch for 1½ minutes; chill in ice water. Drain and pat dry. Pack and freeze.

Quick Look	
Storage	up to 12 months

Celery and/or Carrots. Wash and slice as desired. Blanch for 3 minutes; chill in ice water. Drain and pat dry. Pack like-sized pieces of celery and carrots together or separately and freeze.

Kale. Wash leaves. Fold in half lengthwise and slice off long tough stems; chop remaining leaf portions. Blanch for 2 minutes. Chill in ice water; drain and pat dry. Tray-freeze on parchment paper-lined baking sheet for 30 minutes. Pack and freeze.

Okra. Wash and remove stems of pods without exposing seed cells. Sort by size; blanch small pods for 3 minutes and larger pods for 4 minutes. Chill in ice water; drain and pat dry. Cut crosswise or leave whole. Tray-freeze on parchment paper-lined baking sheet for 2 hours. Pack loosely and freeze.

Onions. Slice or chop as desired *(no blanching needed)*. Tray-freeze on baking sheets until firm. Pack and freeze. *(For longer storage, wrap in foil first before placing in bags.)*

Onion Rings. Slice onions and separate into rings. Blanch for 15 seconds. Chill in ice water; drain well. Coat with flour and dip in milk. Coat again with a mixture of equal parts cornmeal and pancake mix. Spread out on parchment paper-lined baking sheet and freeze for 2 hours. Pack with plastic wrap between layers and store in freezer. To prepare, deep-fry in 375° vegetable oil until golden brown.

Peas. Wash and shell peas; rinse again. Blanch for 2 minutes; chill in ice water. Drain and pat dry. Pack and freeze.

Snow Peas. Wash pods and blanch for 2 minutes; chill in ice water. Drain and pat dry. Pack loosely and freeze.

Turnips, Rutabaga or Kohlrabi. Wash well; peel and slice as desired. Blanch for 3 minutes; chill in ice water. Drain and pat dry. Pack and freeze.

continued

continued from page 59

Vegetable Soup

- ❖ 2 T. vegetable oil
- ❖ 2 C. chopped onion*
- ❖ 2 C. sliced carrots*
- ❖ 1 C. sliced celery*
- ❖ 6-7 C. chicken broth or stock
- ❖ 2 C. diced tomatoes*
- ❖ 2 C. diced potatoes*
- ❖ 2 C. sliced green beans*
- ❖ 1 C. whole kernel corn*
- ❖ ½ C. chopped kale*
- ❖ Other vegetables as desired*

- ❖ Salt and pepper to taste
- ❖ 1½ C. fine egg noodles
- ❖ ⅓ C. chopped parsley*

In a large pot over medium-low heat, heat oil. Add onion, carrots and celery. Cook until vegetables start to soften, stirring occasionally. Stir in broth, tomatoes, potatoes, green beans, corn, kale and other vegetables as desired. Season with salt and pepper. Bring mixture to a boil. Reduce heat and simmer, partially covered, until vegetables are almost tender, about 30 minutes. Stir in noodles and simmer until tender. Stir in parsley. *Makes about 12 cups.*

* Use frozen and/or fresh vegetables and herbs – no thawing necessary.

NOTE *If preferred, prepare soup with fresh vegetables and freeze soup mixture before adding noodles. To prepare, thaw soup in refrigerator and transfer to a large pot. Stir in cooked noodles and simmer until heated through.*

Veggie Combos

Spicy Stir-Fry Vegetables

- ❖ *1 T. canola oil*
- ❖ *4 C. assorted frozen vegetables, partially thawed*

Spicy Sauce

- ❖ *½ C. vegetable broth or zucchini juice**
- ❖ *2 tsp. cornstarch*
- ❖ *2 tsp. soy sauce*
- ❖ *1 T. canola oil*
- ❖ *½ tsp. sesame seed*
- ❖ *¼ tsp. red pepper flakes*
- ❖ *¼ tsp. salt*
- ❖ *Cooked rice*

In a large skillet over medium heat, heat 1 T. oil. Add vegetables and stir-fry until crisp-tender. Meanwhile, in a small bowl, mix broth, cornstarch, soy sauce and 1 T. oil until smooth. Add sesame seed, red pepper flakes and salt; mix well. Stir sauce into vegetable mixture and bring to a boil; reduce heat and cook until thickened. Serve over cooked rice. *Makes 4-6 servings .*

Sweet Variation. Replace the Spicy Sauce with Sweet Sauce. Mix ⅓ C. cold water, ½ C. pineapple juice, 1 T. cornstarch, 2 T. soy sauce and 1 T. brown sugar until smooth. Stir sauce into vegetable mixture and add canned pineapple chunks. Finish cooking as directed above.

* Thaw frozen zucchini juice and use it as the liquid in stir-fry sauces or soups (see pages 34-35).

Fun Freezes

Frozen Fruit Cups. Combine 2 C. each diced peaches, bananas, strawberries and blueberries; sprinkle with sugar. Add 1 can each mandarin oranges, crushed pineapple and fruit cocktail, drained. Thaw and stir in 1 (12 oz.) can frozen orange juice concentrate and ¾ C. lemonade concentrate. Spoon into small plastic cups, cover with foil and freeze for up to 3 months. Thaw until slushy before serving.

Fruit Sorbet. In a saucepan over medium heat, mix 2 C. sugar, 1 C. orange juice and 2 T. lemon juice. Cook and stir until sugar dissolves; remove from heat. Puree 4 C. sliced ripe fruit (peaches, strawberries, raspberries or cantaloupe) and add to sugar mixture. Pour into a 9 x 13" pan, cover and freeze. Working in small batches, process frozen puree in a food processor or blender until fluffy. Ladle sorbet into freezer containers, leaving headspace. Seal, label and freeze for up to 3 months.

Strawberry-Limeade Drink Cubes.

Puree sweetened strawberries. To ¾ C. puree, add ¾ C. sugar and 1 C. lime juice. Mix well and freeze in ice cube trays. To serve, add 2-3 cubes to 1 C. cold seltzer water, lemonade or lemon-lime soda; stir to combine.

NOTE *Peel and slice firm bananas; dip in lemon juice and tray pack to use in smoothies. Overripe bananas can be peeled and frozen whole in bags. Just thaw, mash and stir into quick breads and cakes.*

Index

Vegetables